Cash For College
An ABC Guide For High School Students and Parents

by
Doris M. Bruce-Young

Published by

Young Enterprises Int'l, Inc.
5937 16th Street, N.W.
Washington, D.C. 20011
Phone (202) 829-0039 • Fax (202) 829-7809
Credit Card Orders Call 1 (800) 516-9960

ISBN 0-9639490-2-0

Dedication

This book is dedicated to my six wonderful grandchildren, Billy, Adam, April, Jason, Kelli and Ashley. The information contained in this handbook was gathered and compiled for them and students like them everywhere. To their parents, my two sons, William, Jr. and Cornell; and two daughters; Dorrie and Barbara, whose busy lives demonstrate that a handbook like this could save them many hours of searching for this kind of valuable information. To all students and their parents who find themselves in much the same situation with similar needs. To my husband, William C. Young, Ed.D., who with foresight and initiative, compiled and published *The Higher Education MoneyBook for Women and Minorities: A Directory of Scholarships, Fellowships, Internships, Grants & Loans.*

I also dedicate this handbook to the multitude of individuals across the USA, whose many questions about *The MoneyBook* and expressions of gratitude for it, became the catalyst for developing this companion publication. I owe them all a debt of sincere gratitude.

Doris M. Young

Contents

THE VALUE OF A COLLEGE EDUCATION

Going to college is a wise choice. You knew that when you decided to pursue this goal. So don't let difficulties stop you. If you are willing to work hard and remain steadfast in your resolve, you can be successful. A college education can make a tremendous difference in your life.

Let's consider some of the very valuable outcomes to be gained by getting a college degree.

A. You will have more options open to you in terms of career and job opportunities. You will be able to change and improve your life-style to a greater extent. For every degree you earn, your options will increase.

B. A college education broadens your perspectives and enables you to more fully develop all of your talents and capabilities. You will be able to understand and participate more fully in local, national and world affairs. You will be in a

1

position to make a greater contribution toward influencing change and bettering conditions in human lives.

C. Not the least consideration is the ability to increase your earning power. It is a proven fact that the more you learn the more you earn.

The U.S. Census Bureau provides the following information:

Average Annual Earnings, 1992	
High School Graduates	$18,737
Bachelor's Degree	$32,829
Advanced Degrees	$48,653

THERE IS MONEY FOR COLLEGE

More than $42,000,000,000.00 (that's billions of dollars) in financial aid was available in 1993-94 to students for higher education. According to an article in the April 1995 issue of Ebony Magazine $42 billion are available each year. Other publications put the amount of private sector scholarships at $90 billion. There is much literature around attesting to the fact that billions of dollars for college aid are available and awarded annually.

Not generally known is the fact that high income does not always exclude families from qualifying for financial aid. Nor does a family have to give up all savings in order to be eligible. Almost everyone can show some degree of need under present guidelines. In fact, much of the scholarship money in the private sector is given based on merit and various and sundry qualifications regardless of financial need.

There seems to be an information explosion around the subject of "Money for College." Much of it is misleading and designed to lure you into taking out sizable loans or paying for expensive searches. Beware!

With some ingenuity and expenditure of time, you can do your own searching and get better results at very little cost. This handbook is designed to guide you to many free and inexpensive sources of information. In a simple ABC format, information is given in easy to understand terms and guides the family in developing a long term plan that is both simple and effective.

WHERE TO GET THE MONEY

Locating the money is where we shall begin.

A. *The private sector.*

Philanthropy (giving) for higher education cost is alive, well and growing. One well-known publication estimates that it had grown to the staggering figure of $94 billion worldwide in 1990. Other publications state that no one really keeps an accurate account of either the number of organizations or individuals involved, nor of the amounts given. In most of the current literature it is agreed that many millions of dollars are available annually. Many of these dollars are free. No repayment is expected. All however have stipulations and requirements that are not so difficult to meet. Begin your search with your school counselor and librarian. They are aware of many of the local, state and national sources. They have on hand many scholarship directories for your use. Bookstores and other locations offer inexpensive directories for sale. Start early preferably before or during the freshman year to locate as much information as possible. The sooner you start the sooner you will be able to identify those funds for which you may be able to qualify.

B. *Institutions*

Many colleges have donors who make available scholarships, grants and other aid such as tuition discounts. Colleges administer state and federal funds also. During your sophomore year and not later than the fall of your junior year, write to at least 10 colleges that interest you. Request a catalog and financial aid information.

C. *Governmental Aid*

The federal, state, and local governments offer grants, work-study programs and loans. Almost everyone who gets accepted to college is eligible for this aid. A listing of these funds is offered here with information on how to obtain more detailed information.

U.S. Government

Grants

- Federal Pell Grants: need based; $2,000 (changeable annually); no repayment required.

- Federal Supplemental Grants (SEOG - pronounced SOGS): need based; around $4,000 plus; no repayment required.

- Federal Work-Study (FWS): need based; minimum wage rate; no repayment required.

Loans

- Federal Perkins Loan: need based; $3,000 yearly; repay at 5% fixed interest rate.

- Federal Stafford Loan (subsidized): not need based

  > $2,625-1st yr.
  >
  > -$3,500-2nd yr. - repay
  >
  > 8.25% adj.
  >
  > -$5,500-yrs. 3rd & 4th

- Federal Parent Loan (PLUS): not need based; covers gap between cost & need; repay 9% max.

* See Resources & Addresses p.41

FACTS ABOUT **FAFSA**

The Free Application For Federal Student Aid [FAFSA]; get a copy from your counselor or one may come with college application.

An all important form (complete with utmost care, completely & accurately, mail timely).

- Only one form needed. Indicate each college to receive report.

- Mail as soon after opening date as possible, set by government annually (early bird rule applies).

- Determines need based on family income (must use W-2 + tax return information).

- College financial aid officer determines eligibility, college cost and family payment.

- College will check for admission acceptance before responding to student.

- Wait several weeks before making a call to check for receipt of FAFSA.

- Expect a different response time with each college. (Call to check completeness of file).

- Promptly fill requests for more information.

- Colleges have limited resources (Early birds may get 100% of need).

- Notify all colleges of intentions as soon as your decision is made.

Suggestions About Scholarship Applications
(Complete with meticulous care)

- Apply to as many as you feel qualified for (10 or more).

- Meet deadlines and allow time for decisions and responses.

- Make copies of applications and file for future reference.

- Reapply each year unless otherwise indicated.

- Try for others each year if needed.

Make Your Own Luck

HOW THE MONEY IS MADE AVAILABLE

A   <u>Free money</u> that requires no repayment is, of course, most desirable. Scholarships and grants from private sources, institutions and the government have stated qualifying requirements. Therefore we may say that these funds are free with strings attached! Some of these pay all college costs plus, in some cases, living expenses. As a rule, the greater the amount, the stiffer or more specific are the requirements. Fortunately many of these requirements are the same as college entrance requirements. It is well worth the effort it takes to prepare to meet these requirements in exchange for a free or partially free education.

B   <u>Work-study</u> arrangements can be made in a number of ways. Work programs at colleges are available and are usually a part of the financial aid package made up at individual schools. There are also military (ROTC) sources of financial aid; internships; and, fellowships (usually at the graduate level). There is Americorps where work is performed before college and credited to the college of your choice. Americorps credits are usually preferred over a debt created by large loans.

C Government <u>loans</u> are granted at a cheaper than commercial rate and some are guaranteed. In some special cases loans may be forgiven. Loans are obtained from banks and other lending companies. Loans are usually a part of the financial aid package provided by the college. Be careful in choosing loans. Try to create as little debt as possible.

Beware Of Loan Sharks!

FACTS ABOUT FINANCIAL AID

Don't make assumptions, get the facts. Families with $50,000 or less income can readily qualify for aid. It all depends upon who's giving and who's asking. It is a published fact that certain colleges give aid to families with six-figure incomes.

Some other interesting realities:

- Colleges with high tuition and costs usually award more for your need.

- Most students don't pay the full amount as listed.

- Tuition discounts are often given by high cost colleges.

- Most colleges try to meet all of needy student's need.

- Special packages are given at many colleges to certain minorities, smart students, low income students and students with talent in athletics, music, art, theater, etc.

- Public colleges generally have lower costs than private ones.

- Private colleges generally provide more aid.

FACTS ABOUT COLLEGE ADMISSION

College admission is another area where facts are needed.

Public colleges sometimes have open admissions. A high school diploma gets you in and aid is given on a first come first served basis.

Private colleges set their own requirements and usually stipulate higher scores and give aid at their own discretion.

High prestige colleges usually set very high academic requirements. They admit about one third of applicants. Special consideration is given for various and sometimes unusual reasons such as the need to fill in a spot in the choir.

If you really want to get in, apply. You'll never know if you don't try. Either luck or pluck can make the difference.

PREPARING TO QUALIFY

Planning Is Essential

The expression, "It's not the man, It's the Plan," certainly fits this as well as almost any situation in life.

It is truly amazing how our lives turn out so well considering how little real planning most of us do. Many times events and happenstance rule our lives. An anonymous quote seems to fit perfectly here, "Life is not what happens to you, it is rather what you do."

Remember, you are your most priceless possession and yours to do with as you wish. You've probably heard the news stories of millions of dollars lottery winners quickly ending up broke. Common sense tells us that wise planning and some good advice could have prevented this unfortunate happening.

You have in yourself an asset more valuable than any lottery winning ticket. Like a diamond in the rough, polishing brings out the beauty and the true

value that already exists in its natural state. Polishing should not be entrusted to just any jeweler. Only those most loved and trustworthy should be allowed to make decisions about the process.

Planning to make high school a productive and enjoyable time should be a cooperative venture with parents and the students agreeing to work together towards that goal. The following "tried and true" suggestions might prove helpful in the formulation of a plan.

What parents can do:

- Establish and maintain open communication.

- Set aside time daily to talk.

- Provide a place well equipped for study.

- Assist with assignments when needed.

- Provide for tutoring or other help if needed.

- Offer encouragement, especially for difficult tasks.

- Support and praise all efforts and accomplishments.

- Give guidance and be an example in the development of morals and good character.

- Be firm and authoritative when the occasion demands.

- Show respect for the student's opinions, offering a different perspective when needed.

- Make school visits and get to know teachers and staff.

- Volunteer for school and PTA duties.

- Attend school events, especially ones where your children are participants.

- Encourage and support extra-curricular & community activities.

- Know student's friends and their parents.

- Accompany the student to community events.

What the student can do:

- Accept responsibility for getting good grades.

- Accept responsibility for daily, family and household chores.

- Develop and maintain good study habits.

- Devote adequate time for study (3 hrs. daily).

- Make-up missed assignments immediately.

- Complete and turn in assignments on time.

- Always do a little extra.

- Make it a practice to keep parents informed of progress or problems.

- Ask for help when needed.

- Make it a practice to be courteous and pleasant.

- Keep good relationships with teachers, counselors and others at school.

- Participate in extra-curricular activities.

- Participate in community service and other activities.

- Join clubs and organizations that give opportunity for growth.

- Avoid troublemakers and those with poor behavior.

- Stay away from unsafe places and harmful behavior.

- Don't put popularity ahead of principles & good character.

- Confide in parents and other trustworthy persons when in need of help and advice.

- Pursue your goals with vigor.

SETTING YOUR PLAN INTO MOTION

If you were going on a road trip by car a lot of planning is necessary. Agree on the destination and the time it takes to get there. A map and a tour guide are certainly helpful. Talking with others who have already gone on the same trip could give first hand information and helpful insights about what to expect.

Following the road map and consulting with a tour guide would keep you on course and avoid making wrong turns or getting lost. Advice and reminders from knowledgeable persons would also help to ensure a successful trip.

Imagining that high school is a tour can make planning more realistic and meaningful. So, off we go through high school land.

THE FRESHMAN YEAR - FROSHVILLE

Now that you're a high school freshman, it's sort of like visiting a new town. Things are a bit different here. You'll meet new people and do different things. It will be fun and you'll learn a lot.

Your counselor will be your tour guide. He/she will make sure you have the right courses and help you choose electives that best suit your career goals and interests. Be sure to participate in extra-curricular activities of your choice. Don't forget community activities - church, civic and social.

Advisories and Reminders to Students

- Grades and activities are now recorded in your high school record (Transcript).

- Grades you make now figure into your grade point average (GPA).

- Grades you make now determine your class ranking.

- Make up any deficiencies or low scores immediately.

- Choose extra-curricular activities that fit your talents and interest. (Athletics, music, art, drama, writing, mathematics or science clubs, etc.)

- College and scholarship committees are interested in good grades, special talents, community service, leadership abilities, awards, etc.

- The librarian can help you to explore careers and learn about different colleges.

Parents and Students Together Can:

- Compile information on scholarships, colleges and careers.

- Keep records of courses taken, grades made and report cards, etc.

- Keep albums and scrapbooks.

- Visit sites and persons in the career of your choice.

- Visit a nearby college or colleges.

THE SOPHOMORE YEAR - SOPHTOWN

The freshman year was fun and you learned a lot. Now you are older, wiser and more independent. You'll do many things you did last year, only you'll be better at it. There will also be new and different things to experience. You'll still need your trusted tour guide.

Check with counselors about the basic courses and electives. Be sure you're on the right route.

Advisories and Reminders

- Prepare to take the Preliminary Scholastic Achievement Test (PSAT).

- Ask counselor & librarians about any summer programs at colleges. Some colleges have special ones in art, music, athletics, writing, drama, etc.

- Browse through college directories that profile different colleges.

- Make a list of colleges that interest you most.

- Go to college fairs.

- Take the PSAT. If your scores are high, you'll hear from colleges.

- It is better to get a "B" in hard courses than an "A" in easier ones.

- It is better to improve on a strong talent than to experiment with others.

- It is better to become a leader in one activity than participate in many.

Together, parents and student can:

- Find out more about scholarships and grants.

- Visit colleges, college fairs and job sites.

- Decide on summer camps and/or jobs.

- Be involved in community activities.

- Keep records, albums and scrapbooks.

THE JUNIOR YEAR - JUNIOR JUNCTION

You're moving ahead. You're more confident of your abilities, stronger in your special talents and still growing in independence. This year you'll start making important decisions about your future and learning more adult skills.

Stick with that tour guide/counselor. Stay with the right courses and electives. Check out the advisories and reminders.

Strong Advisories and Gentle Reminders

• Retake PSAT? Take SAT Prep?

• Try for the National Honor Society & also try for Who's Who.

• Write for information from any colleges you might choose.

- Remember a 3.0 GPA and a 1000+ SAT are required by some prestigious colleges and some scholarship committees.

- Remain active in school and community.

- Cut your list of colleges to about 5 or 6.

- Identify scholarships and grants that you plan to apply for.

- Take advanced placement (AP) courses if you can.

- Take the SAT and or ACT.

- Attend college representative's assemblies when they visit.

Parents and Student Together Should:

- Schedule college visits and or visit colleges.

- Write for scholarship applications.

- Learn to use a checkbook & checking account.

THE SENIOR YEAR - SENIOR CITY

This is the big year. Major decisions will be made. Deadlines must be met. If you have stayed with the plan, much has been done already and your tasks will not be rushed or difficult. This should be a very enjoyable year.

Your trusted guide/counselor is more needed than ever. By now you know each other well and are ready to complete the necessary applications and other activities for college admission.

Major Advisories and Urgent Reminders

- Take SAT II Subject Tests soon after courses are finished (optional).

- Retake SAT and or ACT if desired.

- Decide on at least 3 colleges and send applications for admission. (One "Reach" college, one "Sure" college, and one or more "Maybe" colleges).

- Make copies of the applications for the purpose of practice to avoid errors and erasures on the final copy to be mailed.

- Practice writing the essay if one is required.

- Practice interview skills and techniques.

- Identify a counselor, teacher and community person for letters of recommendations.

- Fill out and mail college applications in December or earlier.

- Copy the FAFSA form for practice and mail as soon after the opening date (around Jan. 1) as possible.

- Make copies of scholarship application forms. Practice, to ensure accuracy. Finalize and mail early enough to meet all deadlines.

Parents and Student Together Should

- Obtain W-2 forms as early as possible and file income tax forms.

- Complete and file all application forms.

- Review all forms for accuracy, neatness and completeness.

- Make copies of all forms and file for safekeeping.

- Check all recipients of information to be sure it is received.

- Check college for completeness of student's file.

- Make final decision.

- Notify chosen college and those not chosen of your decision as soon as possible.

A MAJOR CLUE:

Being polite can save embarrassment and regret.

Be careful of the words you speak,

To keep them nice and sweet.

You never know from day to day,

Which ones you'll have to eat.

- Anonymous

CLUE UP!

- Don't be a clone. Valuable things are one of a kind, rare finds, originals.

- Avoid the echo virus. Form your own opinions, think for yourself.

- You're too good looking to look like everyone else.

- Following the crowd sometimes causes a stampede.

- Learn by other's mistakes or you may die young.

- Getting there safely is worth the time you take.

- Trouble can be avoided by following the detour sign.

- Time is a limited resource, spend it wisely.

- "Hang Outs" are for people headed nowhere- people with time to burn.

- "Cut-ups" just need to cut it out.

COLLEGE CAMPUS, USA

Congratulations! You made it! You're glad you kept those records. They made it easier to fill out all of those forms, right? The next 2, 4 or more years will be a time for semi-independent living. Just a few more suggestions, hints and reminders might prove helpful. The following are offered for your consideration.

Things To Take With You

BEDROOM

❑ alarm clock and a pillow to put it under ❑ mattress pad ❑ sheets ❑ pillow cases ❑ blankets ❑ bedspread ❑ under bed storage boxes/ bins ❑ wall decorations ❑ posters ❑ family pictures ❑ waste basket ❑ lamp ❑ small broom ❑ dust pan ❑ clothes hangers ❑ over door hangers ❑ towel rack ❑ small iron

DESK ITEMS

❑ calendar ❑ calculator ❑ dictionary ❑ thesaurus ❑ grammar book ❑ bible ❑ ruler ❑ stapler ❑ glue ❑ tape ❑ paper clips ❑ stationery ❑ stamps ❑ typing paper ❑ notebooks ❑ theme paper

GROOMING

❑ robe ❑ shower shoes ❑ towels ❑ shower tote bag ❑ soap ❑ shampoo ❑ tooth brush & paste ❑ hand mirror ❑ comb & brush ❑ curlers ❑ lotion ❑ sanitary supplies ❑ first aid kit ❑ manicure kit ❑ sewing kit

LAUNDRY

❑ mesh laundry bags ❑ detergents ❑ spray starch

FOOD

❑ eating utensils ❑ wet naps ❑ non-perishables-meats, crackers, nuts, fruits ❑ energy bars ❑ pop corn/popper

MISCELLANEOUS

❑ umbrella ❑ boots ❑ sneakers ❑ exercise clothes ❑ swimsuit ❑ flashlight ❑ trunk/foot locker, locks & keys.

ORGANIZING TASKS SAVES TIME AND ENERGY

When studying, taking tests, or doing almost anything, a good way to make the task easier is to divide a large task into smaller parts.

Start with the simple and progress to the more complex. Do the easier tasks first. The sense of accomplishment propels you in the process of taking on the harder ones. Once you get the momentum going you're in the mood of progressing through the entire process without procrastination or dread of doing what seemed to be a huge undertaking.

Let's say you have a big pile of dirty dishes to wash, you can start by separating the glasses, the silver, the plates, and the pots and pans into piles. Begin with the glasses, the silver, then plates saving the pots and pans for last. This gives a systematic approach for handling the job and making it more manageable than just washing each item as it is picked up haphazardly.

Let's also take the same approach to handling a pile of clean laundry. Separating like items into piles, towels, socks, underwear etc. before folding and putting them away is a more orderly and less time consuming process than just taking each item from the mixed pile.

This same process can be applied to prioritizing which subject to study first when there are assignments to be done in several subjects. Considerations of the amount of time, degree of difficulty and any other pertinent factors should help to make the decision easier.

A test consisting of true/false, multiple choice and essay may be handled in the same way. Usually it is best to do the less difficult and less time consuming items first.

STRATEGIES THAT WORK IN DIFFERENT SITUATIONS

Study

- Make study your first priority, that's why you're there.
- Find a time and place with minimum distractions.
- Have everything you need handy so disruptions don't occur.
- Organize tasks and materials.
- Do the most important assignments first.
- Allow plenty of time and concentrate.
- Consider a study group for certain assignments & projects.
- Be clear about what the assignment is.
- Plan to take short breaks, but not too frequently.
- Review, check closely for errors, re-write, perfect.

Social

- Don't rush into relationships, choose friends wisely.
- Stick to tried and true beliefs and principles.
- You will have to resist becoming entangled in situations and relationships that will not be to your best interest.
- If you are not interested don't waste time being nice.
- What will make you happy and what will distress you are major factors to be considered.
- Do not forsake morals and principles to be accepted or popular.
- Keep your balance and exercise your best judgment in light of your values and educational objectives.
- Don't act impulsively, think it over, sleep on it, seek the advice of someone you trust.

Safety

- Stay aware and alert, paying attention to your surroundings at all times.
- Avoid being alone in deserted places, where people are not about, or out.
- Don't go out alone after dark, stay in well lighted places.
- Don't accept rides with persons you don't know well.
- If a vehicle seems to be following you, quickly go in the opposite direction to a safe area. Call police.
- If you have to walk between buildings at night, ask a security person to walk with you.
- If you are in trouble, attract attention anyway you can. Scream, wave etc.
- Know that the possibility is that unexpected things can happen in unexpected places.
- Stay alert!

Dating

- Traditional dating is becoming outmoded, passé, awkward and sometimes dangerous.
- Group dating is becoming popularly accepted as the preferred way for the opposite sex to associate with each other.
- Getting acquainted and deciding if you're interested is done in a more natural setting with no strings attached.
- The danger of being pressured to become intimate is avoided.
- Each person pays for their share.
- Enjoying the company of one's friends and getting to know a certain person saves limited time.
- Misunderstood expectations can be avoided and a one on one interaction can take place.
- The danger of date rape is removed.

RESOURCES & ADDRESSES

U.S. Government

- The Student Guide, U.S. Department of Education, P.O. Box 84, Washington, D.C. 20244. Call 1-800-433-3243, Free.

- AWARE (A P.C. based software program - encourages high school students to focus on their education). Free. U.S. Department of Education, Application System Division, PSS, Room 4640, 400 Maryland Ave., S.W., Washington, D.C. 20202.

- Preparing Your Child For College (a resource book for parents), U.S. Department of Education.

For Minorities and Women (Inexpensive)

- Young, William C., The Higher Education MoneyBook for Women and Minorities: A Directory of Selected Scholarships, Fellowships, Internships, Grants and Loans. Young Enterprises International, Inc., 5937 16th Street, NW, Washington, D.C. 20011 - (202) 829-0039 or 1 (800) 516-9960.

- Clayton, Martin, The College Reference Guide For African American Students, P.O. Box 49547, Chicago, IL 60649. Phone (312) 643-5389.

RECORDS

Keeping accurate records is a necessity. The forms on the following pages are included to provide a handy space for recording information that will prove useful and readily available. The information recorded here will be needed in many instances in the years to come.

MY FRESHMAN RECORDS

Course Full Name	Grades						Teacher
	1st Advisory	2nd	Semester	3rd	4th	Final	Notes	
1.								
2.								
3.								
4.								
5.								
6.								
7.								

* Required - English, Math, Science, Soc. Science, Language & Electives

EXTRA CURRICULA

Activity	Position Played or Held	Outcome or Award	Supervisor/Coach
1.			
2.			
3.			

44

My Freshman Records

Community Activity/Service

Organization	What You Did	Outcome or Award	Supervisor/Leader
1.			
2.			
3.			
4.			
5.			

Membership In Clubs/Organizations

1.		
2.		
3.		

Summer Camp/Jobs/Other

1.		
2.		
3.		

45

My Sophomore Records

Course Full Name	Grades							Teacher
	1st Advisory	2nd	Semester	3rd	4th	Final	Notes	
1.								
2.								
3.								
4.								
5.								
6.								
7.								

* Required - English, Math, Science, Soc. Science, Language & Electives

Extra Curricula

Activity	Position Played or Held	Outcome or Award	Supervisor/Coach
1.			
2.			
3.			

46

My Sophomore Records

Community Activity/Service

Organization	What You Did	Outcome or Award	Supervisor/Leader
1.			
2.			
3.			
4.			
5.			

Membership In Clubs/Organizations

1.		
2.		
3.		

Summer Camp/Jobs/Other

1.		
2.		
3.		

47

MY JUNIOR RECORDS

| Course Full Name | Grades | | | | | | | Teacher |
	1st Advisory	2nd	Semester	3rd	4th	Final	Notes	
1.								
2.								
3.								
4.								
5.								
6.								
7.								

Required - English, Math, Science, Soc. Science, Language & Electives

EXTRA CURRICULA

Activity	Position Played or Held	Outcome or Award	Supervisor/Coach
1.			
2.			
3.			

48

MY JUNIOR RECORDS

COMMUNITY ACTIVITY/SERVICE

Organization	What You Did	Outcome or Award	Supervisor/Leader
1.			
2.			
3.			
4.			
5.			

Membership In Clubs/Organizations

1.			
2.			
3.			

Summer Camp/Jobs/Other

1.			
2.			
3.			

MY SENIOR RECORDS

Course Full Name

Course Full Name	Grades						Teacher
	1st Advisory	2nd	Semester	3rd	4th	Final	Notes	
1.								
2.								
3.								
4.								
5.								
6.								
7.								

* Required - English, Math, Science, Soc. Science, Language & Electives

EXTRA CURRICULA

Activity	Position Played or Held	Outcome or Award	Supervisor/Coach
1.			
2.			
3.			

MY SENIOR RECORDS

COMMUNITY ACTIVITY/SERVICE

Organization	What You Did	Outcome or Award	Supervisor/Leader
1.			
2.			
3.			
4.			
5.			

Membership In Clubs/Organizations

1.		
2.		
3.		

Summer Camp/Jobs/Other

1.		
2.		
3.		

COLLEGE DECISIONS

Name of College	Address & Phone #	Info. Request Date	Info. Received Date	Rating (1st, 2nd, 3rd, etc.)
1.				
2.				
3.				
4.				
5.				
6.				
7.				
8.				
9.				
10.				

COLLEGE DECISIONS

Name of College	Location (City, Town, Rural)	Size (Lg., Med., Sm.)	Distance (Near-Far)	Cost (High, Med., Low)	Rating (1st, 2nd, 3rd, etc.)
1.					
2.					
3.					
4.					
5.					
6.					
7.					
8.					
9.					
10.					

COLLEGE DECISIONS - 1ST CUT

Name					
1.					
2.					
3.					
4.					
5.					

2ND CUT MAIL APPLICATIONS

Name	Date Mailed	Transcript *Sent (Date)*	FAFSA *Received (Date)*	Response *Received*	Response *(Yes, No, Wait)*
1.					
2.					
3.					

FINAL DECISION

College Chosen	Acceptance Mailed	Orientation Visit	Entrance	Dorm Assignment
1.				

Mail letter of non-acceptance to:

SCHOLARSHIP & GRANT APPLICATIONS

Name & Address	Date Applied	Response
1.		
2.		
3.		
4.		
5.